PHILLY GIRL

Top (L) Jan, her mother and older sister Faye at Spring Lake, New Jersey, near Philadelphia, age 9. (R) Jan in front of her home, age 8. Bottom (L) Jan as a cheerleader in high school (R) Jan, husband Dennis, Jesse age 5, Sam age 2, at the beach near San Francisco, California.

Philly Girl

Janice E. Shapiro, Ph.D.

Copyright ©2019 Janice E. Shapiro, PhD

All rights are reserved by the author. Except for brief passages quoted in newspapers, magazine, radio, television, internet review, or academic paper, no part of this book may be reproduced, stored in or introduced into a retrieval system, or transmitted in any form, or new use, without the prior written permission of both the copyright owner and the publisher of this book.

All inquiries concerning performance, adaption, or publication rights should be addressed to Publisher@PalmDrivePublishing.com. Correspondence may be sent to the same address. Send electronic versions of reviews, quotation clips, feature articles, and academic papers in hard copy, tear sheets, or electronic format for bibliographic inclusion on literary website and in actual archive.

Back Cover photograph, shot by Andrew Sullivan ©2017

Published by Palm Drive Publishing, Sebastopol CA 95472
Email: Publisher@PalmDrivePublishing.com
Library of Congress Catalog Card Number: 2019945791
Shapiro, Janice E., 1950-2018
    Philly Girl / Janice E. Shapiro
    p. cm.
    ISBN 978-1-890834-22-7 (print)
    ISBN 978-1-890834-23-4 (eBook)
1. Autobiography 2. Memoir 3. Philadelphia 4. San Francisco 5. Women's Studies

Printed in the United States of America
First Printing, August 2019
9 8 7 6 5 4 3 2 1
PalmDrivePublishing.com

In honor of
my father Bill Shapiro
who always believed in me and who loved to write
and
my mother Esther Mirow Shapiro,
a strong independent woman
who always had a great story to tell

Just do the steps that you've been shown
By everyone you've ever known
Until the dance becomes your very own

Jackson Browne, *For a Dancer*

About the Author

Janice Elaine Shapiro was born on September 8, 1950, in Philadelphia, PA. She was a graduate of Northeast High School, Temple University, and Georgetown University. She moved to San Francisco in 1978 and worked as a nurse-midwife at San Francisco General Hospital. After her move to California, she pursued her lifelong dream of earning a doctorate in psychology at Northern California Graduate University. She created a successful private psychotherapy practice in Noe Valley, which grew and thrived for over 30 years. She was an integral member of the Rhythm and Motion community at the Oberlin Dance Collective (ODC) and attended classes six days a week for over 35 years. She was married for 36 years to Dennis Biroscak and had two sons, Jesse and Sam. After living with cancer for nearly four years, she died peacefully on August 30, 2018. She lived with passion, energy, and humor. She loved life, her family, and intimate friends.

Acknowledgements

Philly Girl began as a series of vignettes that Jan wrote over the last several decades of her life. She had always intended to turn the vignettes into a book for publication. As her health gradually declined (in late 2017), Jan reached out to longtime friend (and editor) Bonnie Gordon for help getting *Philly Girl* into shape to submit to a publisher. Bonnie responded with enthusiasm and encouragement, and collaborated with Jan, both as editor and close personal friend sharing a final project together. I am deeply grateful to Bonnie for helping Jan realize her vision—to tell her life's story as she saw it.

Janet Parker, whose sons grew up with ours, brought another editor's eye to proofreading the stories, and offered both wise advice and encouragement.

I am grateful to our two sons, Sam Biroscak and Jesse Biroscak, for their belief in their mom as a writer and their encouragement and advice to me in the publication process.

When Jack Fritscher and Mark Hemry, partners in Palm Drive Publishing, first read *Philly Girl,* Jack's comment was, "This should be published," and they immediately agreed to take on the project. Mark Hemry produced *Philly Girl* in its present book form, advising and educating me on the details that publishing a book requires beyond the actual writing.

Sam Biroscak, Beverly Patterson, and Mark Hemry contributed to the cover design. Jan's sister Faye DiGiovanni and Jan's friends Mae Wynne, Bobby Caplan, and Barbara Finberg contributed photographs for the book. Bonnie Gordon and Janet Parker helped me select the pictures for publication.

Jan finished *Philly Girl* during the last nine months of her life. During this time and throughout the four years of her cancer treatment, we received tremendous support from our community—relatives, friends, neighbors, Jan's book club, the Rhythm and Motion dance community—the many overlapping circles of friendships that sustained us. And I include the medical community at UCSF and Stanford, the oncologists, symptom management doctors, and angels on earth—the infusion nursing staff. I cannot even begin to tell you how important this network of generous caring people meant to Jan and to me.

Dennis Biroscak
May 2019

Contents

About the Author vii
Acknowledgements viii
Foreword xiii

Time Changes Everything..1
I Remember Papa 3
Paterfamilias..5
The House is Burning Down....................................7
My Mother and the Kosher Butcher 9
Swan Lake..11
You Can Cross 13
Enemas: A Love Story 15
Bunyips Really Exist 17
My Orthodontist...19
My Mother's Pocketbook......................................21
The Truth about Falsies 23
Sweet Sixteen and Finally Been Kissed 25
Not College Material..27
Barbara and Her Mother, Anne...........................29
Mae..33
The Menopause Ward 35
Hyannis: Summer 1969..37
Williams Hall 41
A Unique Global Positioning System 43
Fried Zucchini Blossoms 45
Bonnie 47
Ruth..51
Betty 53
My Favorite Lesbian 57
Two Jesses 61
Jill's Birth 65
The Wedding: Before and After..........................67

My 40th Birthday Present to Myself.................71
Connie 75
Janet..79
A Genial, Genuine Book Club 81
I Stand Here Ironing Italian Cotton Sheets 85
Regrets and Insights...87
One Last Thing: Night Terrors.........................89
Dear Mila 91
Jani's Scrapbook...93

Foreword

Janice and I were friends for more than 45 years. We met as "Philly Girls" and then cemented our friendship in our New York City days in the mid-to-late 1970s. We would walk all over the city together, and wherever we went, Jani would connect with people. There was something about her. She listened. She zeroed in on people with her eyes, her megawatt smile, nodding her head while people talked to her, and in a New York minute people would tell her intimate details about their lives. Life was always interesting and fun when you were in her company.

Jan went on to become a California girl as well. I was sad when she moved to the opposite coast, but we would always get together when she came back east to visit her mom—and we'd have the same epic get-togethers, meeting at some fabulous restaurant (she always did her research!) and talking for hours, catching up on everything.

When Jan was diagnosed with cancer in 2014, she acknowledged a formidable foe, but determined that it would not define her. Over the next four years—through surgeries, hospitalizations, radiation, and various radical treatments—she lived her life and kept her spirits up—with the help of her family and a wonderful network of friends. She kept *moving*. She continued to dance with her beloved Rhythm and Motion community. She worked. And while her diagnosis was a reminder—to her, and to anyone who knew her—that none of us knows what lies ahead, Jani let nothing stop her from continuing to live her life the way she loved to live it. Her hold on life was tenacious. Between her inner strength and her husband Dennis's intrepid research into yet another clinical trial that might save her, I kept thinking and believing, even until the final months, that she might somehow defy the odds and live into her 90s like her mother did. I could not, would not, picture it ending.

But Janice always had another surprise up her sleeve. At the very end of December 2017, she told me about the stories she had been writing. She'd been at it for 25 years, and aspired to turn them into a book. She recognized that she needed an editor, someone to help give it shape. She asked me to work with her on this project. Jan began to send me the vignettes that make up *Philly Girl*. I was astounded. The stories were warm and witty, intimate and evocative. Brutally honest and often hilarious. Pure Janice. Turns out—much to my surprise and delight—she was actually a very good writer. A natural. We worked, back and forth, well into the spring and early summer of 2018. This project brought us closer together than we had been in many years, and it was so meaningful to both of us. I see it as a gift she gave me. And here, in this book, is a gift that Jani gives you, the reader.

Make no mistake. This is not a book about cancer. It is not a memoir about battling an illness, though she alludes to that sorrow in places. Mostly it is a book about Janice: daughter, wife, mother, grandmother. Friend, reader, traveler, listener, healer, foodie, writer. It is a memoir in the truest sense. Jani's memories, from the time she was a child, through every stage of her eventful life.

These stories, these vignettes, demonstrate Jani's passion for living, her grace under pressure, her ability to forgive and accept forgiveness, and her struggle to remember and to understand. They trace the trajectory of her journey—like a dance, she traveled solo, partnered, and with a group. A dancer to the end.

Bonnie Gordon
Spring 2019

Stretch & Kvetch

Dancing is a huge part of my life - it has been for Philadelphians since the days of American Bandstand. Every girl in Philly wanted to be on the show.

We practiced jitterbugging with dogs too as partners' until we could swing simultaneously with "Franny and Crazy leg Phil" - all parochial school kids from South + West Philly. From age 5, every kid knew how to dance. I expand my repertoire every Sat morning at Miss Goldie's school of Ballet. How I paid the $1.25 every week astounds me as Esther had no idea what ballet is.

The first Swan Lake is the music we practice our first recital at Lit Bros - the department store community room. I have a white feathered headpiece and 9 toms white tutu and had to spraypaint my pink slippers silver. All I know is, the tour jété was my favorite step and I could really jump. We had symmetric quartt: but until one day. Suddenly one of the girls looked swollen and sick and in the next thatway month died of "Leukemia". Our quartett shrank to a trio and when "the Dying Swan" played, we

Jan liked to write her initial drafts of stories in long hand on yellow legal pads.

Time Changes Everything

In early 2014, I was happy and healthy, a perky, dance–class-going working girl, excited about my sons' achievements in love and career. Then I found myself facing a potentially life-threatening diagnosis of lung cancer. That was quite a jolt.

When I was a child, I loved to write. What I would write about most was time travel. The same themes would emerge. I would go back in time, switch things around a little, and create a vastly different outcome. These fantasies involved things like choosing *not* to take the bus one day (which exploded, but without me in it) or *not* getting up in time to go to school (which would be blasted by a nuclear attack). Or I might, in my story, introduce myself to someone on the subway (not my normal shy self). And so on. Today I think that I may have written these narratives in an attempt to control one major "what if" outcome. What if the gunman who shot and killed my grandmother when I was ten had missed? What if he had gone somewhere else? What if he had shot himself instead?

What would my life, and my family, have been like if I had grown up without this tragic event? Here are the questions that haunt me:

Would my mother have been so unstable?

Would my father have pursued the writing career that he had so longed for?

Would my sister have spent her high school years hidden in the basement sleeping?

And I wonder about my decisions. I know that escape and exit became my modus operandi for everything.

Would I have become so insanely driven to get out of that morass and chaos and make something of myself?

Would I have changed my major from psychology to nursing, and gone to Whitesburg, Kentucky, in 1972—where I probably inhaled coal dust, possibly contributing to my current illness?

On the other hand, would I have had the courage to approach Dennis in 1975?

In *It's A Wonderful Life*, the angel Clarence kept showing George how, if he had not existed, things would have been different. His brother Harry would never have survived the ice drowning when he was a boy, and ultimately would not have been able to save the ship transporting soldiers in World War II. Mary would have remained unhappy and alone. His uncle would have been institutionalized.

I wish I could go back in time and change *whatever happened in my life* that caused the tumor in my lungs that now threatens my very existence. I wish I could just write a story that includes the moment when that cell mutation occurred—and then do something—anything—so that *it never happened.*

Unfortunately, life isn't a fiction. I can't just write this one away.

I Remember Papa

I still remember, and miss, my father: William Shapiro. He died in 1997. When I light a candle in remembrance on the anniversary of his death, often my sorrow is compounded by another feeling: specifically, missing people whom I love, people who are far away, people who are alive and in my life but, still, not physically here with me to hug me, or pass me tissues, or witness how bereft I feel as the candle for my father burns.

One year when I lit the candle for my father, my husband was in another country, my oldest son was on the other side of this country, and my youngest son was in California but in another city hundreds of miles away. Everyone was living their busy lives, and I was busy too, but yearning to be—in that precise moment—*remembered*. I gazed at the tiny flame, and wished my family were here to eat dinner with me and reminisce about my beloved father, even though they didn't know him the way I knew him. And I reflect: one day I will be gone. I hope that those who love me will light a candle as generations of Jews have done throughout time. But what will they remember?

I hope that they remember my thick, full sandwiches, which I packed in waxed paper for 20 years—*always in the morning* so that the food would be fresh. I hope they remember my oatmeal, warm and creamy and full of golden raisins and brown sugar just the way my mother made it, with milk added for calcium. I hope they remember my cheerful "good morning" even when I slept poorly or felt like shit or dreaded my day. I hope they remember me as a voracious reader—a legacy from my father. He was a high school graduate and an excellent chronicler of day-to-day events, observations, and memories of his own beloved deceased parents. He would be proud that I became a good reader.

I hope they forgive my moodiness and my high drama about trivial things. I hope my children remember the cheerfulness with which I sent them on trips to enjoy their young lives the way I enjoyed mine.

As I write, I think of my father, who pecked and hunted over a manual Smith-Corona typewriter for 70 years and would be pleased that I was following in his footsteps.

Paterfamilias

My father worked nights at the post office, but on his days off, I looked forward to a regular bedtime ritual that we shared. First, we prayed for the health and well-being of our entire family. Next, I would ask him: How old will you be when I am 10? How old will you be when I am 20? And so forth. I remember, at some point he told me that when I got to be *that* age, he "probably wouldn't be around anymore." This was my first explanation of death.

I recall that I cried during these discussions. He did too. Then we would recite the Pledge of Allegiance together, and he would kiss me goodnight.

In recounting this story at a dinner party one evening, everyone cracked up laughing when I got to the part about the Pledge of Allegiance. "Was there a flag?" one friend asked. I said no, deadpan. I didn't *really* understand what was so funny. But I got in the spirit of the evening and laughed as well.

But my laughter soon turned to tears when I suddenly understood: In the 1950s, when I was a young child, my parents were intensely grateful for being Americans. They had an acute awareness of what had happened in Europe during World War II. It was a miracle that there were any Jewish children alive at all, they would tell me. I later came to understand that to my parents, I was a kind of miracle child.

I felt so close to my father during our bedtime rituals. He always took the time to answer my questions about life and death. He was so patient with me. And each time we said the Pledge of Allegiance together, I see now that he was counting his blessings.

The House is Burning Down

There were the usual rules about not playing with matches, but the day I watched my mother almost burn the house down is seared in my memory. I was seven. Esther methodically and hypnotically lit a match to photo after photo and burned each one to ash. I screeched, "We need a fireman!" I screamed at her to stop. There was no evidence that she heard me. I watched her cry hysterically and then finally soften into a trance.

Much later, I came to understand the roots of my mother's pain. One tragedy after another, beginning with the death of her beloved younger sister, Bernice, nicknamed "Bubbles." My mother was 33 and pregnant with my sister Faye when Bubbles died. Over the course of her illness, Bubbles deteriorated even as she got through nursing school. She attended her June 1947 graduation in a wheelchair and then died that same year, in October. My mother had diapered her as a baby, had cared for her as a child, had loved her intensely. It was an unsustainable loss. Forever after, my mother believed her sister died from falling off a horse.

There was another sibling, Norman. My mother's brother was the only one who went to college. Norman studied to become a dentist; then he had a psychotic break and spent the next 30 years in Norristown State Hospital. He died on the streets, schizophrenic and homeless at the end of his life.

My mother's mother—my grandmother—was murdered in Philadelphia. My mother had to identify her body at the morgue. (She took me with her.)

All of these events in my mother's life helped me understand my mother's "strangeness" through the years, her constant hyperanxiety, her episodic hysteria. I always felt compassion for her because of the tragedies that colored her life.

Tragedy continued even after she died. In an odd postscript, my mother's headstone and the headstones of both my grandparents were overturned when vandals desecrated Mt. Carmel Cemetery in Philadelphia in 2017.

My Mother
and the Kosher Butcher

My mother loved going to the kosher butcher. She went just about every day and spent hours there. My father used to joke that she was having an affair with one of the three fat, bloody-aproned, heavily accented Holocaust survivors who shared duties behind the counter and, in a way, he was correct.

My mother lingered in the shop because they *listened* to her. They loved to hear her talk. She opened up to them about everything—trivial or important—and because she was a good customer, and because my mother had a flair for storytelling, they listened intently. Esther must have felt important, valued, *heard*.

The butchers themselves spoke a broken English. They probably only understood about half of what she was saying. But they were nice to her and she loved them. Years after my father died, as she began her slow decline into an infirm old age, the butchers personally delivered her chicken to her at her home. She actually let them in the house. Such an invitation was a rare event.

I have a butcher too—in San Francisco, where I live now. It's not a kosher butcher. But Steve, the meat guy at my market, came to my rescue one day, making me think of my mother and her butchers. There had been a casual conversation. It was about carnitas. One day a few weeks later, when I stopped in to pick up an order, Steve handed me an envelope.

He had typed out a recipe for carnitas, the one he knew I wanted. He had prepared that and put it aside for me. He made sure to look for me on a day he knew I was coming in to pick up my beef cheeks. I had been in a low mood for days, and his gesture meant so much. I think maybe he had sensed my mood. I can't be sure. But I do know that "listening to your customers" can sometimes go beyond what we usually think of as "listening to your customers." I know that, sometimes, small acts of kindness can go further than you think.

Swan Lake

I have always loved dancing, and I have always danced. I have taken weekly classes since I was a seven–year-old, beginning with Miss Goldy's School of Dance in Philadelphia.

On the same block as Miss Goldy's lived Kenny, the boy I had a crush on from kindergarten until sixth grade. Clutching my dollar-and-a-quarter in my closed palm to pay for the dance lesson, I mentally prayed for Kenny to be on his front step, or on the street. I wanted him to see me in my practice leotard and tights! (In second grade, Kenny gave me his ID bracelet for a day, which meant we were boyfriend and girlfriend. At our 20th high school reunion, I reminded him of this fact. He had absolutely no recollection of me, or of Miss Goldy, or any of this.)

The most important element of Miss Goldy's was the recital. We practiced tiptoeing around on our ballet slippers for years to the music of Tchaikovsky's *Swan Lake*. I had no idea what the story was, or why we were told to hold our heads in a certain way, or instructed to dance in total unison. But I do know that the music transported me. It made me feel very pretty and dainty.

My good friend Arlene was also in this class. She had perfect attendance (as I did) until one year, when she suddenly stopped coming to the class. Miss Goldy explained to us that Arlene was "not well." I didn't see her for months, and when she did return to class she looked different. She did not look like her old self. I guess she looked "not well." We both danced, and I kept quiet about how she looked. I kept my questions to myself. I said nothing. Miss Goldy began getting us ready for the recital. Besides practicing our steps, we all had to collect money to purchase our white tutus with tulle skirts, our feather tiaras, and our white tights. We were instructed to paint our slippers silver.

On the day of the recital, we all gathered at the community room at the local department store. My mother and sister came to watch me. Arlene's family came en masse: there must have been 50 of them in the audience. I thought this was a bit odd; Arlene, by now, was dancing with great difficulty, and she looked terrible. We danced our Dying Swan number, everyone applauded loudly, and the tears flowed freely. In fact, people in the audience were *sobbing*. I really did not understand what was going on.

A month later, Miss Goldy announced that Arlene had died—of leukemia. She asked us for a moment of silence to remember "one of our own dying swans" ... my nine-year-old friend, Arlene.

You Can Cross

In the summer of 1955, the "Whip" came around our neighborhood once a week. The Whip was a truck with a rear flatbed converted into an amusement park ride. It cost a nickel, and I begged my mother to let me ride on it. My mother was reluctant. She was afraid I would throw up on it and choke. Finally, I convinced her, and she gave me a nickel to give to the operator. The ride was exhilarating and it gave me a rush. The man gave me a free second ride. I got off the truck and saw my mother across the street. I waited for her to say "It's okay, Jan, you can cross." My life was full of safety guards. There was Mildred, the lady, and Charlie, the kid—both crossing guards whose authority I respected. I always knew to wait for their okay. My mother said, "Okay, Jan" and I ran into the street, right into the path of an oncoming car. The car sped off.

I was bloody—and crying. My mother wasn't wearing her glasses and hadn't seen the moving car. We went to the hospital. She couldn't cope, and *I* had to reassure *her*. The doctor bandaged me up and told me that I would be okay. At that point, my mother said that the car may have been driven by the teenage son of her hairdresser, Lillian. This turned out to be correct.

How she knew the car and the driver, but didn't stop me from crossing into it, will remain a mystery forever. Her conscience bothered her for weeks. In the end, she decided to donate twenty dollars to our synagogue, out of gratitude that

I was all right. Then she went back to Lillian on Saturdays for her usual cut and color.

Enemas: A Love Story

My mother's holistic approach to well-being included giving her children monthly enemas. She checked our bowel movements every day to make sure they were of the correct consistency and, if not, she filled up the enema bag. Don't think of sadistic scenes from *Sybil*, please. It wasn't like that. In my mother's dotty weirdness, she made it a sort of a fun-filled adventure each time.

We were not a musical family but we did know our patriotic theme songs. While the warm soapy water filled up my gastrointestinal system for the colonic cleansing, we sang *My Country 'Tis of Thee*, from beginning to end, and then we counted backwards from fifty to zero. My mother never helped me with my homework: this was her idea of pedagogy.

I always liked the "hold it, hold it" challenge. In my childhood, no one expected much of me, except to smile and be friendly and remember names. But learning to sing patriotic songs, count backwards, and hold on to the enema water until I felt like bursting has served me well in life: I am the queen of multitasking.

Twenty-five years later, when I was about to give birth to my first-born, I recall desperately trying to push my son out during a three-hour, second stage of labor. The letting go and holding on held a paradoxical pull.

Letting go was never easy for me.

Bunyips Really Exist

Most children growing up in Philadelphia in the 1950s and 1960s remember Sally Starr, *Popeye Theatre*, Mr. Rivets, Gene London, and the *Bertie the Bunyip* show. What exactly is a bunyip? In Philadelphia when I was a child, it signified a puppet that had exciting adventures. We used to sing the theme song. We all wanted to be on the show. We hoped to get autographs from Bertie.

As an adult, on a trip to Western Australia, I went out walking in the bush on the Indian Ocean side of the country. Along the trail, I spotted a kangaroo at close range, which startled me, but it hopped away before I could make its acquaintance. Just as my heart rate began to slow, I saw something else that startled me: a sign that proclaimed, "Bunyips may be seen along this trail. Let them go along their merry way."

The native Australians I met explained. A bunyip, they told me, was a mythic and much-cherished entity of the Aboriginal people in the area. I remember wondering at the time if the writer of the Philadelphia puppet show was Australian. Or had been to Western Australia in the 1950s. I even speculated, hyperimaginatively (I admit), that the writer may have shared a foxhole with an Aboriginal person during World War II, heard about bunyips, and had the idea of starting a puppet show starring one—Bertie! And that *is* an Australian-sounding name, isn't it?

My Orthodontist

I gave a tea party for my 16-year-old friend Sofia. The women who were there began to reminisce about a special time they shared with their mothers when they were young girls. I thought and thought, and suddenly it occurred to me: the *only* one-on-one time I had with Esther was on our monthly visits to the orthodontist.

Ernie Plotnick, Esther's first cousin, was an orthodontist. At my mother's request, he agreed to put braces on my teeth, and on my sister's as well. He even gave us a discount! Getting my braces tightened each visit was torture. But what saved the day for me was the post-checkup ritual of going to a luncheonette afterwards with Esther in downtown Philadelphia. We both were excited to eat out in a restaurant. The kosher restrictions stood, but the sugar restrictions were loosened. I always ordered the same thing: tomato soup, grilled cheese, and a chocolate milkshake. On those days together, my mother seemed like everyone else's mother I knew—except for her unshaven legs. And on those days, following those painful orthodontia visits, I almost didn't mind that. Not when we were having an outing!

Ernie Plotnick was handsome and smart and very gentle, even though I despised the braces. Today, I serve tomato soup in martini glasses with grilled cheese sticks for dipping. We toast my straight teeth.

My Mother's Pocketbook

Esther had sunk to a new low. I never ever thought that she would lose her purse—or "pocketbook," as Philadelphians call them. This was her last object of value, the only thing left of the life that she knew as a working married woman with a home, a husband, two children, a job, and a large savings account. First, she left her job. This was quite a big deal as she loved her job working for the city. She was proud of her working woman's wardrobe. The job was close to where she lived. She walked to work almost every day just to save the carfare. She brought her coworkers homemade muffins and cake at least once a week. My father wanted her to retire when he did, at 65, so that they could travel and do things together. She reluctantly agreed. Her life definitely changed after that—probably for the worse. She preferred working to doing just about anything. But they flew to see their grandchildren and they traveled to London and Israel and San Francisco many times. About 15 years after she retired, she became a widow.

I noticed that the style of her purses changed over the years. It was less about style and more about pragmatics—being able to find her checkbook and keys easily. The purse became her symbol of stability and self-care, and continuity. She no longer had a husband, but she had a purse.

Selling the house was her next big loss. It was five years into her widowhood. By the time she sold the house that I grew up in, she had begun sleeping until 10 in the morning, bathing infrequently, taking all day to prepare and eat her morning oatmeal—and she had lost about 30 pounds. Clearly, it was time for assisted living. She clung to her purse but resisted revealing anything about her bank accounts to either my sister or me. She never really trusted anyone.

After she fell and broke her hip—not once but twice—we began to look for the last place for her to live. And as we made preparations, my mother couldn't find her purse! She had never let go of that old purse she loved, given to her by a dear friend. She loved it. I knew then that my mother was giving up. She was feisty and sometimes she could be mean, but that purse had been her constant companion, and she finally let that go too. After that, she lived—purseless—for another two years.

The Truth about Falsies

My flat-chested (but gorgeous) blonde friend Karin and I spent an entire semester of eighth grade experimenting with one last hurdle (we thought) that might finally help us reach our goal of landing a boyfriend—our breasts. Karin and I acknowledged our common shortcomings when we took a dance class together in Broadway jazz. We were both good dancers with long legs and high kicks. But when the top hats went up on our heads, and the satin vest went down over our leotards, we looked more like Fred than Ginger. In anticipation of the class talent show, we took matters into our own hands—so to speak.

We sewed hooks-and-eyes into our flat-girl training bras so we could attach our newly purchased "falsies." In the locker room, we could put them in or take them out. We were very secretive, and the other girls never noticed what we were doing. The boys noticed though! And they were definitely looking! At the talent show, we filled our satin vests—and became immediately popular in the days that followed.

The following summer, Karin grew real breasts. As for me, at summer camp during a junior lifesaving test, my falsies popped out of my bathing suit. They floated forlornly next to my assigned "drowning partner" (and crush du jour), Ricky, whom I was so excited to be "saving." I had to endure his knowing smirks for the rest of that summer, and for all of our subsequent years at that camp.

I probably should have learned a lesson from back in sixth grade, when I used my mother's eyebrow pencil to create a fake beauty mark (to look like Elizabeth Taylor). That "falsie" was revealed the day my classmate Mark rubbed it off and screamed in the schoolyard, "I won the bet!"

Sweet Sixteen
and Finally Been Kissed

A good father and a good first boyfriend can set you up for a lifetime of trusting and loving men. I was lucky that way—and the feelings I have for my husband and two sons are testament to this. My father was a good husband to my mother and a trustworthy father to me. And I was ready for my first real boyfriend: Bobby. He was romantic and kind and sexy as hell—and, boy, could he sing Motown. He wrote a poem about us for my sixteenth birthday and read it aloud at my Sweet Sixteen party, in front of a captive audience of 35 guests: 16-year-old girls and some of their moms.

"We met in the Catskill Mountains
Amidst beautiful flowers and fountains…"

He really wrote "amidst." I loved him for that, and for his bravery in reading the poem aloud. That day, Bobby also gave me a lovely gift: an ankle bracelet. My guests all loved him, cheered him when he recited the poem and when he presented me with the gift publicly. He had taken three buses to get to the restaurant.

I met him at Brown's Resort in the Catskills. Our chemistry was instantaneous. He was a year younger than me, and so I hesitated. When you're a teenager, that year looms large! But he pursued me aggressively. And I loved when he sang along with the jukebox. We slow-danced. He gave me my first French kiss. Decades later, I can still conjure up those first teenage sexy feelings that he inspired. Our love was so sweet and so pure and so real.

He called the day we both returned to the city. He lived away across town and didn't drive. Somehow, we made it work for two years. Our pet name for each other was "Pup"—that's what his older brother called *his* girlfriend. It felt natural and fun for us to have pet names.

My parents liked him. He dressed well. His father owned a clothing store and he really knew style. We never talked about school or our futures or our parents or anything. We never drank or did drugs. We mostly ate enormous corned beef specials and made out on Saturday nights. We would "park" (as they called it) in my father's car and we weren't even deterred after a police officer shined a flashlight in the backseat of the car, where we were gloriously in heat and oblivious to anything but each other. Despite our terror that night, we did it again the next Saturday night.

I resisted going to "second base" (letting him "feel me up") because I didn't want him to know that I was really flat-chested (see "The Truth about Falsies") at the time and wore a padded bra. We waited until my seventeenth birthday and then, we agreed, that would be my birthday present to him.

Eventually, I graduated high school and went to college, and Bobby and I broke up. As a college girl, I couldn't date a boy in high school. Foolish, perhaps. But life moves on, and I did.

Not College Material

It is very difficult to stand out in a school of 4,000 students. My only claim to fame was wearing a cheerleader uniform on game day and sitting way in the back of the 45-student classroom, as we were seated alphabetically.

My grades were mediocre, except in English, so my parents insisted that I take typing as an elective. My young typing teacher was obsessed with Michaelangelo, and she helped me love him too. I wound up writing my senior thesis on "The Homoerotic Elements of Michaelangelo's Sculptures." I also got support from Miss Martyska, an unmarried teacher from an Irish family.

I spent many hours in the library. It was my refuge. I loved reference books, although they could not be taken home. At bedtime, I devoured the classics: *Wuthering Heights*, *Jane Eyre*, *Of Human Bondage*, *To Kill A Mockingbird*, *Les Miserables* (in English). And many more.

Somehow all this reading translated to my being able to write a coherent, persuasive essay for Miss Martyska and she thought, "Maybe she's smart, after all." I couldn't believe that some adult actually took an interest in my school work. She was the only one.

Summoned to the infamous chambers of Cora Horowitz, the high school guidance counselor, she informed me, "*You are not college material*. Please do not waste your parents' money going."

Evidently, I wasn't the only student dismissed this way. In Frederick Wiseman's scathing documentary, *High School*, (produced in my junior year), Mrs. Horowitz is filmed assailing another girl with the same dire verdict.

When I told my parents what Mrs. Horowitz said, not surprisingly they agreed with her. They still thought that I should become a secretary and get married and live happily ever after.

Live happily ever after? I knew their marriage was no picnic, and that my poor, smart older sister Faye had followed their advice and got stuck being a secretary and was obviously miserable.

Fortunately, my friend Janice worked in Mrs. Horowitz's office. She came out one day with my "permanent record" and showed me that my IQ was high, and told me to just ignore Mrs. Horowitz.

Which I did. Even though my grades and SAT scores were mediocre, I applied to colleges. I even forged my unsupportive parents' signatures. I had no idea how I was going to pay for college, but first I had to get in. Temple University basically accepted everyone in those days. I became an Owl, worked in the library to pay for it, and lived at home my first year.

I learned about slimy fraternities and beer, but mostly how much more educated everyone else was. It was time to step up my game and apply myself to school work. Which I did.

Encouraged by my efforts, after working all day, Faye started night school at the University of Pennsylvania. She wound up getting an MBA and I wound up getting a PhD.

I learned that even when people you should respect think you are nothing, they could just as well be wrong. Screw the naysayers!

Barbara
and Her Mother, Anne

I have the best girlfriends. Each one of them came into my life in an unusual circumstance, beginning with Barbara. At age three, she was my very first friend. Our mothers "fixed us up."

Northeast Philadelphia: 1950. The neighborhood was brand new. Predominantly Jewish at the time—poor *schleppers* who moved from Strawberry Mansion, or South Philly, or Kensington. Families who had just enough money to put a deposit down on a first house. Barbara's mother, Anne, spotted my mother—with me in the stroller—as we came out the door, and invited us into her house. Barbara and I are still friends to this day, kind of like Lila and Elena in *My Brilliant Friend*—but without the competition or boyfriend stealing, no malice whatsoever. And her mother became a role model for me; she taught me how to love and be loved. Anne always smiled, was gracious and kind, served nice meals, set the table, and was filled with millions of other little sparkles of sweetness and kindness—so unlike my own home.

When we were 10, Barb and I created a camp for neighborhood kids. We charged each child a dime, which included a Popsicle for lunch. As young preteens, we compared breast sizes. We giggled and made fun of her skinny little brother, Joel. We played "rocket ship" together, using the glittery rocks of my corner house as "planets" to touch and land on.

I learned about Oreo cookies at her house; no junk food was permitted in mine.

Barbara and I used to sneak into her parents' bedroom to read the hidden, illustrated book about "what married women do." We loved this book and would read it together, repeatedly, throughout the years.

Barbara also had the privilege (from my point of view at the time) of going to Hebrew School—which she dreaded. I wanted so badly to be allowed to go too; I wanted a bat mitzvah. But my parents did not think it was necessary for girls to have a bat mitzvah. Barb and I made a deal that she would come over once a week with her Hebrew lessons and teach me everything that she had learned. This lasted about two times. But I wore my first bra to her bat mitzvah party. And at that party, I danced with "older boys."

Something that occurred at that party is a good demonstration of her mother's kindness to me. My mother used to give me a Tonette home permanent every year, and I despised them. I hated the smell of the liquid, the burn on my scalp, and how I looked so ugly afterwards. I did not want to go to Barbara's party with my frizzy look from the dreaded Tonette. Now, as it happens, my grandfather was a barber by trade, and I used to hang around the barber shop where he worked when I was a child. In fact, for a time, I aspired to be a hairdresser. In any event, as a preteen, I was confident that I knew how to cut hair. So before the party, I took my toy scissors and chopped off half of my hair. Anne took one look at my botched haircut the very second I walked in, and took me aside to the bathroom. In the midst of her daughter's bat mitzvah party, she found a pretty bow from one of the gifts, and stuck it on the bald side of my head to hide my inglorious mistake. I have always loved her for that.

Barbara and I had some ingenious projects. Our bedroom windows faced each other. One day, we hooked up a clothesline pulley. We put written messages in a paper cup and then we would pull and pull until the cup went all the way over to each other's windows. It wasn't easy to get this to work though. We created quite a stir among the neighborhood kids, who watched us patiently dropping the rope from her bedroom down to the ground, then try to toss it up two floors to my bedroom window. It took us about 30 attempts to get the rope up through the window. Later, we graduated to toy "princess" phones which, in effect, were walkie talkies. We loved talking before bedtime, sharing secrets.

And we could entertain! Barbara played the accordion and I danced. We called ourselves the Rosey Roses. We performed live with our parents as the audience. We would create little menus listing "appetizers" and descriptions of our songs and dances.

Anne helped me plan my Sweet Sixteen party. She helped me pick out my dress. I would wear that dress today if I still owned it. Silk, bright Kelly green, long swirling skirt cut on the bias for dancing.

I have white Caesarstone countertops because of Barbara. She has exquisite taste, and always finds *exactly* what she is looking for, no matter how long it takes. When I remodeled my kitchen in 2011, she helped me see the benefit of white versus dark countertops—and she was so right. The last time she visited me, she brought one of her beautiful acrylic paintings. I had kept my walls bare for six years, because I liked the tranquility and the lack of visual noise. But that painting became part of my kitchen décor, a symbol of the first friend in my lovely life.

Mae

Mae was my first out-of-the-neighborhood friend. We met when we were five at day camp. She had Shirley Temple curls and dimples. We liked the other campers, but we had so much fun together that we hung around mostly with each other all summer. We lived on the border of different elementary schools, so after camp was over, we didn't meet up again until ten years later in high school.

Mae was one of my high school idols. She rebelled against the stupid dress code by wearing the same thing every single day for a year: jeans skirt (actual jeans, or any kind of pants, were not allowed—ingenious!), white blouse, white socks, and white sneakers.

My mother didn't trust Mae. When we were 15, my mother yelled at her because we wanted to go to the local hangout after 9 p.m. She considered 9 p.m. the witching hour; you don't go out after 9 p.m!

There was a group of us: Janice, Wynnie, Mae, and me. We used to go to People's Drug Store after school to eat fries with salt and ketchup and drink Cokes. The three of them smoked Newports, but I secretly disapproved. At the time, I had very few opinions of my own, and no idea of how to express myself. I admired these girls, each for individual reasons. Janice was a math wiz. Wynnie wore makeup. So mature, I thought! I had no idea why they let me hang around with them. They were the cool girls. In the 1960s, they mimicked hippies—in style at least—beginning with wearing long, loose skirts. But I moved in another direction. I became a high school cheerleader.

My mission was to **not** have to go home directly after school. To achieve this goal, I needed an after-school activity. I was too short for the basketball squad and too skinny for girls' hockey. I did not play a musical instrument so that took care of band. But I could *dance*! So I tried out for the cheerleading squad. In a high school of 4,000, being selected as one of only 12 cheerleaders was a great honor.

I started hanging out with the cheerleader crowd. I had mixed feelings. I really preferred to be with Janice, Wynnie, and Mae. But I was fearful or hesitant about their extracurricular activities, which included smoking pot. On the other hand, my cheerleader cohorts were unfriendly and snobby. I continued to hang out with the cheerleaders, the "popular" girls.

My friendship with Mae somehow survived. She was always game to travel. She was spontaneous and super fun. I learned about sarcasm from her.

We spent time together in British Columbia (where she eventually moved) and became "the American girls" who camped at Sprout Lake on Vancouver Island. I did yoga on a plastic mat and ate cooked brown rice and canned pineapple with chopsticks. She had a number of boyfriends that summer. One was a handsome, blond hairdresser who washed Mae's hair in the lake with Herbal Essence shampoo. Most of those Canadian boyfriends of hers turned out to be gay.

We love each other still. I love pleasing her, and she appreciates every little thing. When she last visited, we had rum and Diet Dr. Pepper—her favorite. Mae is unique—who else loves rum and Dr. Pepper? She still giggles like a girl and goes to rock concerts. No one ever forgets the inimitable Mae.

The Menopause Ward

In 1969, I was a psychology major at Temple University. I wanted some actual real-world experience working with "crazy" people, instead of just reading *The 50- Minute Hour* and visiting my schizophrenic uncle Norman at Norristown State Hospital on Sundays. So I became a nursing aide at the Quaker-founded Friends Hospital, the oldest psychiatric institution in the country.

The landscaping around the building was beautiful—wisteria vines and tulips and rose bushes throughout the well-manicured grounds. Wealthy lunatics were known to take up long-term residence here, and parts of the hospital resembled a country club. The hospital permitted brides and grooms to have their wedding pictures taken on the grounds. High-end photographers brought sophisticated equipment, and the patients loved to watch. Often they would wave from their windows and shout down to the smiling couples in the garden. Sometimes they would yell, "Don't do it!"

I was assigned to what was casually referred to as "the menopause ward." My job was to hand out tranquilizers in the late afternoon and sleeping pills at bedtime. I wore a yellow pinafore and a yellow ribbon in my ponytail. As the new "pill girl," I was automatically popular. The women all called me "Hon."

I walked the patients to recreational therapy, where they made potholders and ashtrays and painted by numbers. I escorted them to physical therapy, where we played volleyball together. The job so far seemed easy and pleasant enough. I was saving money for an end-of-summer vacation with my girlfriends to Hyannis, Massachusetts.

One day the head nurse gave me a new assignment. I was to take the women—most were diagnosed with "involutional melancholia"—to their electroshock therapy treatments.

My job was to hold their hands. And to put straps on their ankles. And to place a padded tongue blade into their terrified mouths. This was not what I had bargained for at two dollars an hour, planned vacation or not!

The huge jolt came, and I nearly gagged, fighting the urge to vomit from the horror of watching my nice, heavily sedated, middle-aged smokers look as if they were being electrocuted. Which they were, in a way. When it was over, I helped them into their wheelchairs and took them back to their rooms. I cried quietly, trying not to let them hear. For two weeks, the women became total zombies. They couldn't remember my name. Now I understood why they all called me "Hon."

Hyannis: Summer 1969

I'd saved money working at Friends Hospital and used it to join my camp/college friend Ellen, who had rented a huge house in Hyannis for the summer. After taking my first airplane on Eastern Airlines to Boston, then Hyannis, I started my first day of work at Howard Johnson's.

We had to buy nurses shoes to go along with the stupid uniform. We didn't get paid for a week, while we trained to make "frappes" and hot fudge sundaes, carry all-you-can-eat fried clams on a tray with one hand, and figure out tax and totals. I was definitely out of my league, especially in the tray-carrying and bill-figuring-out department. I was definitely the worst waitress ever.

It only took me two weeks to get fired. My colleagues were really nice, friendly girls from Smith, Wellesley, and Mount Holyoke, and they said Cape Cod was the summer destination their entire lives. Working at this Howard Johnson while their parents lolled around Wellfleet or Truro in their expensive summer legacy homes was a typical New England, Seven Sisters type of summer. Their boyfriends all worked there too. Unfortunately, I gave one a free hot fudge sundae while off duty and I was immediately sacked. There went my first months' tuition at Temple for the fall.

Fear not: I was intrepid, and landed a job at The Cranberry House as a cashier. Still, my math skills haunted me and I was short at the register every single day. That lasted another week.

Then: maid at the new hotel. Couldn't clean a bathroom—out again. Cleaning girl for a rich guy in Truro—fell asleep on the job. I was basically failing at everything in the Cape. I started to believe Cora Horowitz's predictions about me. (See "Not College Material.") But I did love swimming in the Atlantic, and I met some Kennedy cousins in the ocean who flirted shamelessly. This was the summer of Chappaquiddick and I saw the scandalous effect that it had in Hyannis.

I couldn't lie very well about all of the firings. My father took a Greyhound bus to Hyannis to bring me home. We had lobster for the first time in our lives. He begged me to come home. He said Esther was a wreck hearing about all of my failures (and she hadn't heard about half of them). I said no to Dad. I said that I was never coming home again. I said "home life" was killing me and I had to go my own way. He cried and cried and I saw him take the return bus home. Honestly, it never occurred to me to say yes.

Draft dodgers from everywhere used our big house on the water on Columbus Street as a safe waystation to get up to Canada. There were six of us cute, "hippie-dippy," free-loving girls happy to feed and entertain them. I met and fell for Joey. He liked me but not as much as I liked him. Ellen, the queen bee and organizer of the Columbus Street rental, liked him too. She had huge breasts, was wealthy, a flirt, and a liar. I had always believed her camp-days story about her so-called stepmother being so close to her, yet the glazed weird look in her eyes ultimately revealed her to be a victim of molestation, a girl who harbored a huge desire for revenge. She shocked us all at the end of the summer by ransacking our suitcases of tips (tuition and Williams Hall money for me) and running off. Disaster—everyone left but me and Lynne: we had tickets in August to go to Woodstock, and this was not going to stop us.

We hitchhiked there with no money, no tent, and no plan for the weekend. I was arrested on Route 95 in New London, Connecticut, as a runaway, even though I was 18. Maybe 21 was the legal age at that time. I conned the cops into believing me when I pretended to call home. Actually, I called their own number, got a busy signal, and created a blatantly false conversation with my "parents." I told the police that they approved of my plan to go to Woodstock and that hitchhiking was fine with them. Oh boy. I have no idea how the police believed me but they did.

Woodstock was a total mess. People are pretty impressed when I say I was at Woodstock, but for me, the *only* good thing about it was seeing Jimi Hendrix live. It was muddy, crowded, and unsanitary with few port-a-potties, unruly trippers hallucinating, and nothing to eat. Lynne and I had nowhere to sleep, although some boys offered us money to stay in their tent. We said no and just became a sodden soaking mess until the sun came up and we escaped.

Back on the road. I had lost my shoes in the mud, so I was barefooting on the highway. Scary truckers picked us up. It took us 14 hours to wind up in Framingham, Massachusetts, where Lynne had a furious aunt and uncle who agreed to pick us up. I was so grateful. They drove us to Hyannis the next day and we recovered from the horror of Woodstock. For me, that summer wasn't about love and peace or anything but chaos, hallucination, pouring rain, and being ripped off by Ellen, whom I thought was my friend. Never saw her again.

To this day, I have no idea how I ever came back to Temple with enough money for tuition and room and board to stay in Williams Hall. What I do know is that I learned the only way for me to grow up and survive was to escape and be self-sufficient.

Williams Hall

It was 1969: Woodstock had completely worn me out. My parents could not persuade me to come home after that summer. I moved into Williams Hall, the women's dorm at Temple University, typing Dewey Decimal numbers on cards for the library to pay for my room. On the first day, I met my college roommate, Sue, along with her parents and her boyfriend Neil, who studied music at the Curtis Institute. I have two things to thank Sue and Neil for. First, they gave me a birds-eye view of two people having sex every Saturday night. And second, Neil taught me to appreciate the sound of classical violin music; he practiced all the time. Over the next few years, I came to appreciate Brahms violin concertos and also the proper way to respond to receiving oral sex. Thank you, Neil and Sue, for that!

Then there was Reeva, the smartest person I had ever met. I was unsophisticated and silly, and she hated me at first sight. As dorm switchboard operator, she knew everyone's business—who called whom and who didn't receive any calls at all. She had all the power.

Reeva got to know every boyfriend by the sound of his voice, and the same with our mothers. She would announce one of my suiters: "Mr. Plaid Pants is here—Janice Shapiro." Ouch. She was definitely the mistress of Williams Hall.

That year, we both loved Danny. But Danny had a crush on me, and Reeva wanted Danny for herself. Danny came from Athens, Pennsylvania—absolutely nowheresville, USA. He wore suspenders and saddle shoes and horn-rimmed glasses. He was weird and awkward. He had a stutter. We found the stutter kind of charming. Reeva considered Danny her "project," but he liked me. Soon, he grew out his curly black hair into a white-boy Afro. He lost the saddles and the horn-rimmed glasses. For a while, he followed me around campus. We giggled in English class, and he finally asked me to a Joni Mitchell concert. Reeva was furious.

Williams Hall had a rule in those days: "three feet on the floor." This was to ensure there would be no full-on make-out sessions in our boy-restricted rooms. One night, Danny and I were caught in the act and put before a student tribunal. Reeva gloated, and hoped that I would be thrown out of Williams Hall. That didn't happen.

Here's what did happen: About a month after the Joni Mitchell concert, Danny told me that he was in love with his roommate, Tom. Soon after that surprise, Reeva and I became the best of friends—and remained so for years. She turned me on to John Barth, *The Oresteian Trilogy*, and Tim Buckley. We loved Tim with a passion, and would quote lyrics from his songs all evening long.

Danny stayed friends with both of us. Much later, he would fall in love with yet another Tom—and they've been together for decades.

Reeva died of a brain tumor in 2008. May she rest in peace.

A Unique Global Positioning System

Mae and I spent a summer traveling around the Great Northwest in her 1969 orange Vega. Although Mae had an undeserved reputation as a slacker in high school, she was an extremely well-organized traveler. She knew how to fold and pack things in a car in ways that astounded me. I only knew how to fold the handkerchiefs that I ironed for my father.

Esther was extremely upset about this trip. She thought of Mae as a hoodlum—her word—simply because she had tried to get me out of the house one school night in my senior year after 9 p.m. I viewed Mae as my only real "rebellious" friend, however, and I treasured that friendship in my quest to set myself free from my own reputation as a cute cheerleader with a boyfriend.

I recall the night we were in a hotel room in rainy Portland, Oregon, watching the Democratic Convention on TV together. I was heartsick and homesick that night, and upset about the protests I was seeing in real time. I had felt conflicted all that year: I knew the Vietnam War was wrong and I hated Nixon, but my parents had instilled in me the value of patriotism. They told me we could have landed in a concentration camp had we not been Americans. I was supposed to feel grateful in this safe haven that was America. And yet I felt afraid. Why were parents squared off against their protesting children? I sensed the depth of my ignorance and my naiveté, and my discomfort that evening was all-pervasive. All I wanted was to be an innocent child again. The adventure unfolding on the screen before me was for someone *else*, someone worldlier, more articulate, someone who could debate the issues. I didn't even know how to fold and pack.

Once Mae and I found our campsite on Vancouver Island, however, I relaxed a bit. Canadians seemed nice. Their lives and outlook appeared uncomplicated, like I was at the time. The people I met seemed to have no fixed opinions, no special issues to argue. This was such a relief to me that summer. Our Canadian companions drank tons of beer and watched hockey games. They barbecued salmon. Some invited us into their homes and their boats—and their beds, when their parents were out of the house. I fell for a guy: he looked like a blue-eyed, long-haired cigar store Indian, and was likewise mostly silent. But he was handsome! The romance I wanted that summer was entirely in my own imagination; that "romance" was pure animal lust, but I yearned for something more. I recognized something about myself: I could never have sex without *caring*.

One morning I took my bike on a back road. As I biked downhill, a truck hit me. I don't remember the moment of impact. Neurologists later told me that was due to traumatic amnesia—nature's way of deleting a horrific memory. I had no identification on me, however, and so I became a "Jane Doe" at a hospital in Port Alberni, Vancouver Island in British Columbia. I was unconscious—and unidentified. The compassionate Canadian healthcare system had things well in hand. They looked after me until Esther tracked me down, calling the Canadian doctor and sending over my health insurance information. For years, my mother's story was that she contacted the Canadian Embassy and informed them that her husband worked for the American postal service. This was her steadfast explanation of how she had the necessary "clout" to locate me. Mae later told me that *she* had called my mother and told her where I was. But I've always liked my mother's story better.

Fried Zucchini Blossoms

When I was not quite 20, I met a boy who made me fried zucchini blossoms. He found me at a commune in New England, populated by lost souls, draft dodgers, closeted gay boys—and me for a few days. It was called the Total Loss Farm, and it was (famously) part of the back-to-the-land movement promoted by Ray Mungo, cofounder of the alternative Liberation News Service. (I didn't know that at the time.) I landed there after the Jeep that had picked me up hitchhiking overturned in the snow; the driver had a connection to the farm, and he had the good sense to deposit me there while he dealt with the chaos that had just erupted in his own life on that wintry, snowy day. There I met Robby, who liked me. Later that summer, back in the city, he somehow tracked me down (there was no Google then to aid in that process)—and cooked an entire meal for me. The first course was fried zucchini blossoms. This was the beginning of my evolution as a foodie.

Oddly, I can't recall the exact taste of those zucchini blossoms, but I remember they were delicious. Also, I loved the notion that someone would *cook* for me to win me over. (It worked.) The beauty of the presentation, the originality of the ingredients, the thought and care he put into the meal opened my eyes to a new art form. And, he used *salt*—a brand new concept to me. In my mother's kitchen, salt was only used in the koshering process. As for ingredients, I was trained to eat an apple a day—*baked,* since my mother "didn't believe in" cold food. Somehow, that daily apple managed to put my taste buds completely to sleep.

The exquisite lushness of those fried zucchini blossoms from the butter-yellow zucchini squash seemed to awaken in me a new sensibility, enhancing my sense of taste and smell and fostering an all-around appreciation for food. Forever.

Bonnie

I met Bonnie at a consciousness-raising group on women-only night at the local Y. We talked about being assertive, being strong, about our bodies, and about abortion rights. Afterwards, we swam in the pool naked. We talked about boyfriends and books and sex. You might say we bared ourselves to one another from the outset. We had so much in common. We were both students at Temple University, though I was a year or two ahead of her. One thing that was different was that I lived in an apartment with roommates, while she still lived at home with her parents. She was desperate to move out and be on her own like I was.

Bonnie invited me over to her house, and I met her adorable mother Jean, who fed us Tam Tams with strawberry jelly and hot tea with lemon. We still eat that when we are together.

The summer after we met, I was accepted into a program in the Appalachians—my chance to "help people." This was an outgrowth of LBJ's War on Poverty, kind of like a VISTA program, but just for nursing, medical, dental, pharmacy, and social work students. I received a small salary, which I badly needed to pay my college tuition and apartment expenses. My plan was to sublet my room for the summer to Bonnie. She persuaded her parents to say "yes" to her moving out "just for the summer." In reality, her plan was for this to be the beginning of an independent life. I was happy to make her dream come true, and thrilled to have a new and trusted friend to take care of my room and my plants.

What neither of us could have predicted was that my ex-boyfriend, Ronnie, would continue to drop in, invite himself to dinners with the roommates, and proceed to fall in love with Bonnie. I didn't mind, but I also felt protective. I knew how Ronnie could be a con artist and manipulator. I knew how he could lie. But I also knew that when I loved him, no one could make me see reason. "Maybe he will be different with my Bonnie," I thought. He had a pattern with women: after nine months, his roving eye kicked in. With Bonnie, the relationship lasted twice as long as his average relationship. But, it still came to the same hurtful, dastardly ending. Bonnie and I became even closer through our mutual commiseration.

For a few years, we lived in New York City at the same time. She showed up at my Brooklyn Heights apartment (shared with Dennis) one day—with vomit all over her. She had gotten sick to her stomach in the subway. I put on my "nurse hat" and my latex gloves and examined her. "Bonnie," I said, "did you know that you are pregnant?" She had suspected it, and nine months later, she was one of the first of my friends to have a child.

After I moved to San Francisco, I returned to Philadelphia every three or four months to visit my mother, first in her home, then in an assistant living apartment, and finally in a series of nursing homes. The nursing homes were near my older sister—30 to 40 miles away from where Bonnie lived, but she always met me somewhere close. We found great restaurants, splurged on extravagant meals, always including a fabulous dessert. We were so happy to be together and we sat for hours over our meals, talking about husbands, sons, previous lovers, work, therapy, books, politics, gossip, hair color—everything. These visits were a boon to my sanity on those four-day weekends visiting my mother, time I spent out of both love and duty. Bonnie helped me find the humor in my mother's rants and her invented stories. She always assured me that I was doing the right thing.

When my mother passed on, my visits to Philadelphia ended. But our love, and modern technology, have kept my friendship with Bonnie solid. These days, Bonnie visits her (still adorable) mother Jean, in her long-term care residence. It's what daughters do.

Ruth

Ruth and I met in a drama class. We were 21. I was a psychology major, but I had to take electives, and I thought drama class would be an easy one. I was wrong. I loved reading plays, but grades were based on assigned monologues.

Petite and curly-haired, Ruth—a theatre major—knew everyone in class. She excelled in sarcasm, and just immediately struck me as "cool." She was assigned "The Girl" in *Our Town*, a small-town innocent, a part that required her to drink a cherry phosphate. I was assigned two monologues—the young girl in *A Taste of Honey* and the heterosexual teacher in *The Children's Hour*. Both are tragedies, and each usually brings an audience to tears.

I was not cut out for dramatic monologues. I flubbed my lines in both. The audience roared with laughter. I had committed the ultimate theatre faux pas—enacting a tragedy and turning it into a full-throttle comedy. So Ruth's first impression of me was terrible.

As time went on, though, we became friends and, later, on-and-off roommates. Ruth had epilepsy, and I had switched from psychology to nursing, so I sort of knew what to do when she had a seizure. Her mother, Ena, depended on me to report any occurrences to her. She and I also became friends.

Ruth and I began baking, using the Tassajara Bakery cookbook as our guide. Ruth never let me cut the cheesecake cookies because she is exacting, and I am sloppy. We still have that dynamic. I accept her, and she accepts me.

We once took a crazy trip together to Key West. The captain of a boat invited her on an overnight, and I went along as the wingwoman. We thought we would have another grand adventure, but it didn't turn out that way. The guy was a creep. We should have gotten off the boat, but somehow we did not have the words at the time, or the self-confidence to say "no." Today, so many of us have learned how to trust our "creep" vibes and say "no" when necessary. But in those days, Ruth and I did not really have the word "no" in our vocabulary. In fact, we didn't know anyone who did.

Betty

I first got to know Betty in 1976 in the New York City Health and Hospital system. The city hospitals were about to hire freshly minted nurse-midwives to supplement the surge of foreign-trained obstetricians who frequently insisted on performing C-sections for the Puerto Rican, Colombian, Dominican, Salvadorian, Panamanian, and Haitian patients. The nurse-midwives were expected to act as buffers between the foreign doctors and their black and brown patients, who expressed themselves during their labors in very culturally specific ways—screaming and wailing rituals, for example—which we midwives were somewhat used to. It was a good plan. The women learned to trust the nurse-midwives, and they got wonderful, personalized care.

Betty was a talented African American woman from Brooklyn, who was familiar with the clinic in Bedford Stuyvesant and could navigate the Bronx Concourse. She knew how to stay calm, read a fetal monitor, help a woman with her labor, and deliver babies with ease. Meanwhile, I was petrified all the time, and kept taking the subway in the wrong direction. She was a calming influence, and I became a better professional with her guidance.

We became close friends, and bought season tickets to the New York City ballet. We loved the magical environment of the Lincoln Center for Performing Arts, a perfect antidote to the dungeon-like chambers of the NYC Health and Hospital system.

We also worked together at a clinic in Williamsburg, before that location became the hip enclave it is today. In the mid-1970s, it was populated mainly by Hasidic Jews, African Americans, and Dominicans. They lived in the same neighborhood but kept a wary distance from each other. And they all loved the "lady midwives."

The Hasids called us by our last names. "Here comes Shapiro," they would say. No man or non-Jew was ever permitted to touch them, so even though I was a secular Jew, they insisted on being cared for by me. Then there were the Spanish-speaking patients, who evidently thought I was hilarious when I tried to communicate with them in my high school Spanish. When they complained about aches in their abdomens, I would suggest they use a warm towel to relieve the pain. But I used the word *caballo* (horse) instead of the word *toalla*. So I was telling the women to put a "warm horse" on their pregnant abdomens. What could be funnier? Every time I walked into Williamsburg Clinic, the women would giggle and point and sometimes convulse in hysterical laughter. Our Spanish translators never ever corrected me. On my last day, they admitted that they just loved to hear me amuse the patients by mashing up their language.

Betty guided me through my own labor with my firstborn son. Three hours of pushing is enough—for anyone. My baby just wouldn't come out. Betty, Dennis, the doctor—all were in the room encouraging me, but absolutely nothing worked. We all stood under the shower, we all got on the floor, we all screamed and breathed together. I was fully dilated for three damn hours, but no baby.

The doctor walked out of the room for a second. Betty started tweaking and pulling at my nipples. That did the job. "Here he comes!" she said. Then, "He's crowning!" She ran for the doctor, but really I wanted Betty to deliver the baby herself. I knew from watching her as a colleague that she was so damn good at it. I needed her calm and stoic nature. But she returned with the doctor. He got the baby's head out, and then the newborn's heart rate dropped precipitously. I was terrified. I knew that meant impending doom. I prepared myself to have a stillborn.

"Three cords around the neck and a *true knot*," the doctor shouted. I was crying and sweating and pushing. No one could have predicted this dire circumstance, but my brain told me a dead baby was coming. My experience as a midwife was that this was the only expected outcome when the umbilical cord is wrapped around the neck three times. It had to be quickly unwound in the correct direction—almost impossible, I knew—and it was a "true knot," which was strangling my baby. I heard the doctor say: "Shoulders out, now body, cord unwound. Dennis, do you want to cut the cord?" *Oh my god ... maybe he is alive.*

There was no sound for a full minute. Hilary, a glamourous nurse with scented perfume and a perfect manicure, worked like a dog to get Jesse to "pink up." Betty worked right alongside her. Finally, finally, Jesse started to cry limply. We *all* started to cry—deep sobs of disbelief and shock, gratitude and relief. Jesse was tiny (6 lbs, 5 oz), and he must have been starving in utero with that tight knot. Betty reassured us that he would be okay, hugged Dennis, and stayed with the baby. Betty, Betty, Betty— thank you!

My Favorite Lesbian

I have always had a special connection to lesbians. They have been drawn to me, and I to them—and in at least one case, a lesbian changed the course of my life.

In fifth grade, my friend and neighbor, Janet, tried to hump me when she spent the night at my house. I found this experience to be quite pleasurable. I remember she told me that I would make a wonderful nurse or doctor. Janet became pregnant at 17 and was kicked out of our high school. Although I am not gay (and I guess she really wasn't either), I will always think of her as the one who lit the fire to my sexuality.

Two years later, when I was moaning through a terrible case of the mumps, my mother asked me what I would like to read. I told her that I was interested in the Civil War, and she unwittingly bought me *The Carpetbaggers* by Harold Robbins. It was full of page after page of hot and stimulating trashy sex. This was part two of my sexual awakening.

The closeted girls in camp found me on sleepover nights when we were allowed to swim in the nude—buckbathing, we called it then. Donna F. groped me year after year in the dark pool and always picked me first for the volleyball and softball games, even though I was a mediocre player. Favoritism? You be the judge!

I always enjoyed this physical attention, but had no idea what was going on. I had no words at the time to explain to myself why the girls (and not the boys) were touching me but I questioned nothing, and accommodated anyone who showed an interest in me.

Jean M., my college roommate, fell in love with me and expressed her love by befriending my boyfriends, and even sleeping with them. She admitted as much. That friendship did not end well.

A fortuitous lesbian connection occurred around the time I was accepted into a nurse-midwifery program at Georgetown University. I was offered a fully paid scholarship plus a stipend for living. The glitch? I had just moved all of my stuff to British Columbia, where my friend Mae lived. I'd planned to move to Canada and live there forever. Instead, I accepted the program's offer and made immediate plans to celebrate this new direction by going to Kauai the next day with Mae.

Mae had a friend in Maryland, Laurie, who promised to pick me up at Washington National Airport when I arrived in DC and to house me until I found my own apartment in Georgetown. When we called Laurie, she mentioned that her friend, Dennis, might be coming by Mae's house soon, as he was backpacking through British Columbia and she had given him Mae's address as a contact.

Indeed, a postcard from the mysterious Dennis soon arrived to say that he would be coming by her house in the next day or so. We left a note on the door saying that we were going to Kauai, sorry.

Later, when I made the move to DC, Laurie met me at the airport. She let me know that she was missing the end of *Marjorie Morningstar* on TV, but since I was Mae's friend, she would make the sacrifice. Laurie and I became good friends. She nicknamed me Thumbelina, and we frequently went into paroxysms of silly laughter singing the song together. She confided in me that she loved a girl named Terri, but Terri hadn't slept with girls yet. I think maybe Laurie thought that I was gay too. Laurie also mentioned a guy named Dennis, who was her friend and sometimes her lover. She said she didn't want to hurt him by leaving him for a girl, but she really wanted to pursue Terri. Did I have any advice? I told her to go for it, even at the risk of Terri's rejection.

On December 19, 1975, Laurie held a birthday party for all of her friends at the Pines of Rome restaurant in DC. It was the coldest day of that year. She showed up for about a minute, and then announced that she was going to the airport to meet her friend Terri. She instructed everyone to meet and mingle until she returned. The strangers at the party stared at each other for a while and did their best to comply. At some point during that evening, a cute skinny guy who I saw staring at me ambled my way. I broke the ice and said "Hi." Shy-guy said "hi"—and then there was silence. Finally, I introduced myself as Laurie's friend Jan. He said, "Hello, I'm Laurie's friend, Dennis." This was the same Dennis who we left the note for in British Columbia, and the same Dennis who Laurie was trying not to hurt so she could be a lesbian with Terri. This was the Dennis whom I found amazingly attractive, and I said, "I'd love to talk to you sometime."

By the way, Laurie never returned to her party.

Two Jesses

When I first met Dennis, I realized that we had very different styles of communication. He was reserved. He thought before he spoke. He was contemplative and quiet. He was oriented in logic. He was cautious. But I was none of those things. I was impulsive. I *blurted* out my thoughts. I was creative and silly. I was steered by my emotions. My words were two steps ahead of my thoughts, thoughts that were often outside the box to begin with.

Our conversations needed a lot of tweaking. For two years, we struggled with a series of verbal misunderstandings between us. A profound physical connection kept us together, but ultimately (but not *ultimately*!) we split up. It was not amicable.

I moved on. My conclusion at the time was that I needed a Jewish man (which Dennis was not). My expectation was that a Jewish man would "get" me in some way that, at the time, I felt Dennis did not. My post-Dennis dating life became *only Jewish men need apply*, and they must understand the "blurt." I sought a fast talker, a fast thinker, someone who could keep up with me in that area. My vision quest in San Francisco led me to one Jewish man after other, but the best of the group was a 19-year old man named Jesse.

I was 30 at the time. But I don't think we ever discussed our ages. He worked at my local fruit and vegetable stand, and he knew how to pick the perfectly ripe banana. He had just returned from a year on a kibbutz in Israel—how Jewish is that?—and before that he had lived in London. A mother lost to cancer, a father (who he lived with)… well, his father had Majolica dishware!—immediately I was in love. I had never before eaten an artichoke. Jesse served me one on a plate *shaped* like an artichoke.

Jesse was leaving soon to go back East to study Russian at Bard College. He was sexy and silly like me, and he teased me in a goofy "Frenchified" English. He was smart and literary, and he wore glasses. I was only attracted to guys who wore glasses. Oh, and of course, there was that Jewish thing.

But he wasn't Dennis.

Jesse moved back East. The romance had been short and sweet. Before too long, Dennis and I rediscovered each other. He had a mission too at that time: *to win me back* by becoming my new "best girlfriend." It worked. We have been married now for 36 years.

Here's an interesting twist. More than 25 years later, I was online reading a review of a new piece of writing by… my old young-boyfriend Jesse. At least, it was the same name. Could it be him? I Googled him and learned that it was indeed him, and that he had become an author and a Russian translator who worked for the United Nations. I wrote to him by postal mail on my professional letterhead (didn't want him to think I was a stalker!). He confirmed his identity and soon acceded to my request that he reach out by phone so we could catch up. He told me about his wife and children, the books he had written, and his job at the UN. I told him about my oldest son, *Jesse*, who was coming home from Dubai in two weeks. I mentioned that my Jesse spoke French and Arabic and needed a job. Older Jesse said the UN needed someone with those skills. He suggested younger Jesse stop off in New York for an interview that he would arrange. My Jesse got the job, worked there until he started graduate school (his UN credentials were key!)—and all because, back in the 1980s, I thought I needed a Jewish man who would be a "blurter" like me.

And yet another twist: Many years later, "older" Jesse started inviting my now-grown Jesse to his famous Passover seders. Older Jesse's Greenwich Village kitchen is so cool that it was once featured in the *New York Times* Food section. My charming handsome 24-year old Jesse happened to be seated that night next to an interesting, older woman, Susan, who insisted that Jesse meet her "brilliant, gorgeous, 24-year old" communications officer at the Brennan Center for Justice in New York, which she ran. Maggie had graduated from Brown University and the London School of Economics and (said Susan) "I *know* in my heart of hearts that you two will be a match." My Jesse said, "Fine." Convincing Maggie was another story. "No way was I going on a blind date arranged by my yenta boss," she said. Finally, she relented. *One blind date only*, she said.

They met; he was late. Jesse wore a Fresh Prince of Bel-Air tee shirt. Maggie was charmed and amused. Drinks became dinner—and that was 10 years ago. They are happily married and have a darling two-year old, my granddaughter, Mila. And I have my former "19-year-old boyfriend," Jesse, to thank—again.

Jill's Birth

New York City, 1979. Dennis and I were in a restaurant in Chinatown when a man choked on a chicken wing. I pulled him in front of me and did a Heimlich maneuver. He was fat and very rigid. Finally, the bone popped out of his mouth. The diners broke into applause.

As if that were not enough excitement for one night, while we were putting on our coats to leave, the manager asked for our name, and said there was an urgent phone message. It was Carmen, my brother-in-law, telling us that my sister Faye was in labor. He asked us to take the train to Philly as soon as we could.

We arrived at 30th Street Station at about 10 p.m. in freezing sleet. It was slippery and bone-cold. The lone cabbie took us to the Hospital of the University of Pennsylvania and there was my sister, in deep labor. I covertly did a vaginal exam on Faye and learned that she was eight centimeters dilated, a great sign that the labor was progressing quickly—and I expected her to deliver with ease. I felt the baby's head with my gloved fingertip and knew that she would have curly hair.

Four hours later, Faye's labor stalled, but finally my niece was delivered at 2 o'clock that morning by Caesarian section. By now, Dennis, Carmen, and I were starving. We went to Pat's Steaks (whiz, wit') in South Philly to celebrate the birth of my beautiful curly-haired niece, Jill Ann DiGiovanni—who would ultimately become a vegetarian. Her loss!

The Wedding: Before and After

In 1982, Dennis and I decided to get married. He had been living and working in Saudi Arabia. He came back to San Francisco, and to me, a changed man. He learned that it was futile to advise, push, nag, or even suggest anything to me, unless he could completely disguise it. He was wily about this. He had given much thought to our past failures and was determined to save me from my worst self. We started running together.

Among other things, he decided to quit smoking, a precondition on my side for our getting back together. He did it cold turkey when we vacationed in Tahiti shortly after we reunited. He sweated out tobacco and coughed up green gook. But we walked and swam and snorkeled and ate croissants and drank fabulous French coffee. He has not touched a cigarette since.

By now, we were living together, and we planned to have a wedding in our own backyard. We planted grass and some trees, rented some folding chairs, and invited 50 of our friends and his parents and mine—meeting now for the first time. He built a special ramp to transport his wheelchair-bound mother on the day of the wedding. We hired a rabbi—he looked like Moses!—who was willing to marry a Jew and a (lapsed) Catholic.

I was still dancing—always dancing—in a class called Rhythm and Motion, developed by professional dancers for people like me—nonprofessionals who simply love to dance. The music always had a great beat, the class was fun, and I got a reliably good workout. I loved these classes and needed them; they were my healthy "addiction." I went with my two actress friends, Faye and Janet. At that time, I was a nurse midwife and teacher. (Sometimes I would bring my students to class. We all had beepers and sometimes they went off simultaneously, letting us know a woman was in labor at San Francisco General. Off we would go. Dancing had to wait.) Sometimes, after class, we would head straight to Just Desserts for the perfect chocolate cake, feeling justified that now we could make room for those calories.

On the morning of my marriage to Dennis, I went to an 8:30 a.m. Rhythm and Motion class to steady my nerves. Faye and Janet were both scheduled to take part in the wedding—Faye was to hold one part of the chuppah (made with my mother's tablecloth) and Janet was to announce to the seated guests that the ceremony was about to begin. She would also signal to Faye's boyfriend to begin playing the cassette we had chosen (*Chariots of Fire*) for our wedding processional music.

The wedding was called for 10 in the morning on a Sunday. Chronically late, I came trotting in to my house at 9:45 a.m., sweating, still in my dance clothes. I had to shower and change into my sister's wedding gown—lent to me for the occasion—which had a million little cloth buttons on the back! I spotted all of my guests in the garden and got the giggles as I rushed to be on time to my own wedding. Dennis stood outside greeting guests, in an all-white tuxedo and white ankle boots, dressed like John Lennon on the cover of *Abbey Road*. He was grinning from ear to ear, and he looked both super silly and ridiculously handsome. He reassured each guest: "Yes, Jan just came back from her dance class, she will be here any minute. Don't worry!"

Here's what sticks in my mind from that day: my mother asking me if I was sure of my decision (I was) and my father asking me if *all* of the rabbis in California wore their pajamas to officiate (it was a caftan).

I remember that Dennis was happy and cheerful in a way he saves for special times. This was a special time. I remember saying "I do." The church bells at St. Paul's down the block rang out just as our service ended, and everyone shouted "L'chaim!"

My 40th Birthday Present to Myself

Following the Challenger explosion, NASA sought to recruit former employees who had demonstrated stellar work. Dennis was one of them. This was 1988. We lived in San Francisco and owned a home, had two sons ages 3 and 6. I said no. No, no, no... I loved it here, my kids had friends and we had friends, and I had finally become a psychotherapist with a thriving practice. I had earned that degree at night, writing papers until the wee hours, and working full days as a nurse midwife at SF General, leaving me sleep deprived. No, I said.

NASA was begging Dennis to come back to Goddard Space Flight Center in suburban Maryland. So it was him or me. We went to couples counseling for a year, trying to resolve this. Finally, I said yes. We sold our four-room dump in Noe Valley (now worth 3 million dollars), bought a custom house in Silver Spring, Maryland, and arrived one week to the day before the Loma Prieta earthquake struck San Francisco—and split our old house in half.

Montgomery County, Maryland, had a wonderful school district, neighborhood pool, and tons of kids. Jesse had a ball. But there was nothing for me or Sam. Nothing. The school bus picked up Jesse so there was no meeting other parents. The Cub Scout parents just dropped off their kids, and Dennis became de facto cub leader. From my huge house, I watched the leaves on the trees turn beautiful colors, with nothing to do all day. There was no state reciprocity for my marriage counselor license. I had nowhere to go. I was depressed and miserable and I just roamed around Montgomery County looking for a decent cappuccino.

There was a local Mrs. Fields cookie café with a Faema espresso machine. I became excited that this would be my new place to sit, and sip, and figure things out. But the counter people refused to learn how to use the exquisite machine. I wrote to Mrs. Fields herself, explaining the waste of a $10,000 machine that her employees wouldn't use. She had someone take the machine back. Now what?

I started applying to PhD programs in the DC/Virginia/Maryland area. I figured Georgetown would accept me, as I was an alumni. They didn't. I took night courses in statistics. I applied everywhere. I was an experienced therapist by then; surely someone would accept me into a clinical psychology PhD program. But no. I was rejected by every single one: evidently, they wanted young male research types, not middle-aged mothers. I almost ran my car into a pole; that's how low I had become, thinking that my life had come to this. Nothing to do, nowhere to go, no one to talk to.

Fortunately, I had kept my San Francisco office phone number. My former San Francisco State professors had started a freestanding counseling psychology PhD program and they invited me to start in September. Quickly I formulated a plan: get Jesse into a decent school for the fall, start the program, restart my practice, and find an apartment to live in with the kids while Dennis looked for a job back in San Francisco.

But then Dennis couldn't find a job, and Jesse was rejected from every decent school. I was forced to make a "Janice's Choice": Go back to San Francisco with one kid and save myself, or kill myself in Silver Spring, Maryland. I went back with Sam.

I arrived on my 40th birthday, started my PhD program the following week, reopened my practice, and rented a one-bedroom apartment. Jesse was "excited" to have Dennis to himself, he said. We flew him cross-country every six weeks *by himself* at age six on United, and he was fine with that. At that time, you could escort your child to his seat, meet the assigned flight attendant, and have the other parent meet the arriving flight to welcome your child. For Jesse, it was a grand adventure. To my current and past San Francisco friends, I was both Jezebel and Joan of Arc: How could I abandon a child and husband for my own need to work and advance myself? Was I divorcing Dennis? What the hell was I doing?

I answered to no one, as usual. My father couldn't get me to come home from Hyannis when I was 19 and no one was going to make me languish as a bored depressed housewife in Silver Spring, Maryland. I just didn't care what anyone else thought about this decision.

My 40th gift of giving myself a meaningful life is one of my proudest moments. Twenty-seven years later, when my patients say, "I picked you because you have a PhD," I have myself, and, of course, the dastardly Cora Horowitz (see "Not College Material") to thank.

Connie

In 1988, Connie and I bonded over our screaming babies in Drewes Meats, the oldest butcher shop in San Francisco. We were poised, professional women in our thirties—how could these screeching, inconsolable babies belong to us? How could this have happened? We stared at each other in recognition. She was begging her three-month old infant, Dalia, to calm down, and I was likewise imploring my 18-month-old toddler, Sam, to quiet down. "Everything's fine, here's a toy, here's your bottle, take my shiny keys"—anything to get each of them to quiet down while we got some ground chuck.

Nothing worked. There was crying and laughter (moms and babies both), and we bent over our strollers like we were kissing the Pope's hand, but nothing worked. Nada.

"I'm Connie," she said, in that warm, soothing tone of hers that can spin a story so long, so anecdotal, and so full of fun characters, interesting details, and absurd observations. She also roared like a lion when she laughed. "I'm Jan," I said, "and this is Sam, my pain-in-the-ass younger son."

I was in hot water and so was she. These screechy, colicky babies were driving us insane. Going out in public terrified us. We both became accustomed to people staring: mothers of screaming babies are looked at like they are criminals and batterers. "Is everything alright?" well-meaning strangers would ask.

Noooooo! I hate my kid, and I hate my life. I get no sleep, no respite from this grouchy midget. I was sure this baby hated my guts—why else is he screaming all the time? I never said that aloud. Just: "Everything's fine—he's just tired" (hungry, bored, wet, whatever you can think of at the time).

So, this is how Connie and I became friends. We thought of ourselves as good mothers and reasonable, kind, empathic people. It turned out we both worked part-time as therapists. She had a half-time job at Kaiser but wanted to start a private practice. "I just found an office in our neighborhood," I told her. "It's pretty nice, decent rent, part time." Just what she needed. She moved into the office next door to mine. We were office mates for 30 years, and it never got stale. It was fun and amazing—a shared journey of glory and tragedy.

Connie's story is somewhat mythical. I have heard it many times, and each time I think of magical realism. For example, her parents are Colombian, and her father was a general in the Colombian army. Her mother worked in a box factory. There were four siblings, but only Connie was born in the United States, when her father came to UCLA to get a master's degree. She recently visited her childhood home in Bogotá. That former residence is now a fancy restaurant.

Speaking of fancy restaurants, I almost lost my Connie because of one. We go out to dinner a lot, and it was my turn to pick a place. I found what I thought was a new pop-up in a café near my dance class. My restaurant radar was off that night. We walked in, and everyone was wearing heels, tuxedos, fancy clothes. We were dressed supercasually. The waiters started pouring champagne and we were served an amuse-bouche, but by the third course, with yet another glass of wine, I realized that we were in the wrong place. I asked the server what pop-up this was, and why they kept pouring us different wines, which we were not ordering. "Oh, this is Saison," he said (the most expensive restaurant in San Francisco), "and you are eating a nine-course meal with a wine pairing." "*Stop*," I said…"no more wine." Connie was pissed.

This was 30 years into our friendship, but I had hit a nerve that night. I always knew she had a temper, but it had never been directed at *me*.

She had compromised as a child, living with an abusive alcoholic father who loved his wife and children in spite of his disease. She accommodated her husband by having a full-time job when she really wanted to work part-time so she could pick up her kids at school, pack their lunches, and help with homework. She gave in when her husband wanted to live all around the world, though she preferred to stay in one place so that the family would have the stability that she never had as a child. That night at the restaurant, she had had it: no more accommodation! Her patience had run out. The pleasant, amiable girlfriend I thought I knew showed me her impatient and angrier self. But she was right; I had not been paying attention, and I had blown it. I offered to pay the $350-per-person bill. I expected her to accommodate to my mistake, but she let me know she would not. How could I have been so dumb? I apologized. "I made a mistake," I said. "I am so sorry. This will never happen again."

Connie lost a beloved sister to cancer, and that left a hole in her heart. But my world-traveling, story-telling friend is still a fun person to hang out with and remains an emotional open book.

Janet

I met Connie at an actual meat market, but I met Janet at The Meat Market Café. It was 1978. I had just arrived in San Francisco, thinking that everyone only read books about astrology. Janet was with her best friend, Faye, who was reading Joan Didion's *A Book of Common Prayer*.

The two of them were inseparable, and I became the third buddy. We ate a lot of Just Desserts chocolate cake, laughed hysterically at Faye's unstoppable drippy nose, which she always wiped with one of her *schmattas*. We were three Jewish girls from back east who had all escaped a proscribed boring future. Janet and Faye were in a theatre company together, and for money, Janet was a taxi driver and Faye drove a van for disabled people. Faye eventually moved back East and later died from brain cancer. We still miss her and love her. Janet and I became a twosome then, always sensing that empty seat at the table for Faye.

Janet is seriously the most private person that I have ever met. No one really knows what is going on inside her mind. This used to frustrate me, but she is always there for the people she cares about—and even for those she doesn't care about. She drives old ladies to synagogue, volunteers at a literacy nonprofit for small children, plays a serious game of Jewish Mahjong, and belongs to a great book group. Janet always put others at the top of her list. She would drop what she was doing for anyone who needed something. Janet *always* shows up.

Regretfully, I have not always been there for Janet. I see now that I could be undependable and unreliable. I have changed over the years. My friends Janet and Bonnie taught me the importance of being dependable and reliable. I came to recognize that excuses, and hemming and hawing, are not adult behavior. I was frequently unavailable for my friends, routinely putting work and my kids before everything and everyone else. I never watched Janet's children during a family crisis, when her father died suddenly on a cruise ship in Morocco—and the Moroccan government wouldn't let the family recover the body.

Eventually, we identified certain issues that had divided us: judgmentalism, criticism, competitiveness, status, differing intimacy needs. It took 10 years, way before my cancer diagnosis, to work out all of the details of what went wrong. Our friendship deepened dramatically and was cemented from then on.

For the last three years, she has accompanied me to my wig stylist every month. We continued to talk about all those issues that we had not previously addressed. At this point, we have discussed and forgiven each other everything.

We sit in a quiet, private room and we tell each other the truth. Janet writes down my requests for my memorial on her yellow pad and I know it will be exactly as I wish. I can always depend on my dear Janet.

A Genial, Genuine Book Club

I have been part of a book club since 1990. Members have come and gone over the decades but there are always six to eight of us—a group of genial women who genuinely love to read. Once in a while, a new member joins us—sometimes they stay, or sometimes they turn out to be bossy, insisting on a change to our agreeably successful format, and eventually the outlier leaves. It's like a blind date—sometimes it just doesn't work out.

We are an eclectic bunch, and we've been through a lot together. Three members have lost their husbands, four have had (or have) cancer, one has had a stroke, one lost a grandchild, one completed a doctoral program while continuing to be part of the group each month. We are, by profession, therapists, attorneys, archivists, artists, and one restaurant owner. Our adult children have become nurse practitioners, realtors, government techies, art gallery curators, architects, and teachers. Many of us have traveled all over the world. We have brought cakes, soup, and full meals to each other in times of illness and grief. Our members hail from Morocco, Spain, Colombia, and Yankton, South Dakota! We are conflict-avoidant, in a good way, and we never ever have arguments, even about books. We may, of course, *disagree*.

We are resourceful. One year, we tried to find the definition of a Latin word used by Michael Ondaatje in *The English Patient*. We were at Jane's house—she was one of our most brilliant readers, but she had to leave about 10 years ago. (I miss her.) Jane looked in every dictionary that she owned, including the Oxford English Dictionary. Eventually, she called her librarian mother in Massachusetts. Her mother actually *knew* the word, and gave us the definition, off the top of her head.

Recently, my dear friend Bonnie, a former English major (none of us were English majors), and now an editor, visited me on a weekend that I was to host the book group. She attended as a guest, the first time we ever did that. She brought a lot to the group with her "English major" type insights—who knew about "the omniscient narrator"? Not us. It was a great group that day.

Wendy keeps track of all of our choices over the years. Our very first book was *One Hundred Years of Solitude* by Gabriel Garciá Márquez. Our all-time favorite: *A Fine Balance* by Rohinton Mistry.

Each of us is an avid reader, who escaped into reading for hours and hours as girls. Each of us has turned to literature for comfort, for transformation. We love the story, we appreciate the tone, the voice, the style, and the point of view. We like to step outside of our lives, into another world that the books create.

We take turns selecting a book for the group to read. We might do research on the author. We may find reviews of the book and interviews with the author. We preside over a narrative thread and we elicit opinions from one another. We are artful and diplomatic in our guidance. We are a sensitive lot, but we try not to take it personally when a member dislikes our choice of a book.

Sometimes it is a challenge to get a consensus on a meeting date or even a choice of a book. But we've been reading together for 28 years, so we've obviously overcome that challenge on a regular basis.

Some of us are friends outside of group, some not. There is a sweetness and positive energy every time we meet. We would do anything for each other, and we have. We love to read together, and we fundamentally enjoy each other's company. How great is that!

Some of our other choices over the years:

- *Love in the Time of Cholera* by Gabriel Garciá Márquez
- *Palace Walk* by Naguib Mahfouz
- *Humbolt's Gift* by Saul Bellow
- *Herzog* by Saul Bellow
- *My Brilliant Friend* by Elena Ferrante
- *A Manual for Cleaning Women* by Lucia Berlin
- *A Gentleman In Moscow* by Amor Towles
- *White Teeth* by Zadie Smith
- *Americanah* by Chimamanda Ngozi Adichie
- *Patrimony: A True Story* by Philip Roth
- *American Pastoral* by Philip Roth
- *The Human Stain* by Philip Roth
- *Indignation* by Philip Roth
- *The Orphan Master's Son* by Adam Johnson
- *Let the Great World Spin* by Colum McCann
- *Atonement* by Ian McEwan
- *Nutshell* by Ian McEwan
- *Olive Kitteridge* by Elizabeth Strout
- *My Name Is Lucy Barton* by Elizabeth Strout
- *Anything is Possible* by Elizabeth Strout
- *Crossing to Safety* by Wallace Stegner
- *Angle of Repose* by Wallace Stegner
- *The Color of Water: A Black Man's Tribute to His White Mother* by James McBride
- *The Good Lord Bird* by James McBride
- *The Underground Railroad* by Colson Whitehead
- *The Things They Carried* by Tim O'Brien
- *In the Lake of the Woods* by Tim O'Brien
- *The Goldfinch* by Donna Tartt
- *The Secret History* by Donna Tartt
- *The Emperor's Children* by Claire Messud

- *The Presidents Club* by Nancy Gibbs and Michael Duffy
- *Between the World and Me* by Ta-Nehisi Coates
- *Midnight's Children* by Salman Rushdie
- *Down and Out in Paris and London* by George Orwell
- *A Moveable Feast* by Ernest Hemingway
- *The Paris Wife* by Paula McLain
- *Interpreter of Maladies* by Jhumpa Lahiri
- *The Namesake* by Jhumpa Lahiri
- *White Noise* By Don DeLillo
- *The Year of Magical Thinking* by Joan Didion
- *Slouching Towards Bethlehem* by Joan Didion
- *Bastard Out of Carolina* by Dorothy Allison
- *Hillbilly Elegy* by J.D. Vance
- *The Tender Bar: A Memoir* by J.R. Moehringer
- *The Duke of Deception: Memories of My Father* by Geoffrey Wolff
- *The English Patient* by Michael Ondaatje
- *The Handmaid's Tale* by Margaret Atwood
- *Evicted* by Matthew Desmond
- *No Ordinary Time* by Doris Kearns Goodwin
- *Team of Rivals* by Doris Kearns Goodwin
- *Wait Till Next Year* by Doris Kearns Goodwin
- *The Social Animal* by David Brooks
- *Undaunted Courage* by Stephen Ambrose
- *The Road* by Cormac McCarthy
- *Room* by Emma Donoghue
- *Gilead* by Marilynn Robinson
- *The Lovely Bones* by Alice Sebold
- *The Devil in the White City* by Erik Larson
- *Lolita* by Vladimir Nabokov
- *To the Lighthouse* by Virginia Woolf

I Stand Here Ironing Italian Cotton Sheets

Give me expensive Italian cotton bed linens and I am a happy sleeper. I like them ironed, with a faint scent of verbena linen water. Freshly ironed Italian Frette linen—so cool, crisp, and clean. Sleep on these sheets and it's as if you are in a five-star hotel, but in the comfort of your own home. I spend an entire day washing my Frette sheets in special Victoria's Secret Laundry detergent (which, sad to say, has been discontinued). I time the dryer cycle so that it is still damp when I start ironing. I take out the spray bottle of linen water and take my time, ironing and spraying. It is a meditation. I become silent and calm, pleasurably anticipating that night's sleep. Crawling into bed and experiencing ... perfection.

One summer in Naples, traveling with my son Jesse, I spotted Frette linens at a fantastic price! But we were late for our train to Pompeii, and my son pressed me forward. I regret passing up what seemed to be an irresistible bargain. I wished for a second pair of sheets, so that when I spend my entire day washing and ironing my beloved first pair, I could replace them with a nice clean second pair. There was no time to buy that second pair that day, and so I only have the one set. In my final days, I hope to be on a clean cool ironed set of Frette sheets. Let me drift off gently into that good night, with the faint scent of verbena water in the air.

Regrets and Insights

Once I thought that I would live to be 99 years old, like Esther. Now, if I make it to 68, I will be the luckiest person in the world of people with lung cancer—metastasized lung cancer.

Everyone asks me if I am afraid or angry, or both. What can I be angry at? My shitty bad luck? My genes, one wildly out of control? No reason for that. I am purely and simply sad.

Cancer feels like an uncontrollable alien, an animal out of control within my body. I can't reason with it to stop its invasion. I can't sweet-talk it into submission. I just have to accept the time that I have and realize that life can change on a dime, as it has for me.

I won't get to see my beloved granddaughter Mila go to kindergarten, read aloud by herself, tie her own shoelaces, have her first boyfriend (or girlfriend), go to her first boy/girl party. I won't attend her high school graduation, or see her in a prom dress.

I won't see my son Jesse become the fully mature man that he is becoming in his early thirties. Won't watch him ripen, become comfortable with his successes as a man, a father, a husband, a son.

I know that I won't see Sam get married, have children of his own, come to me one day and empathize with how difficult child rearing really is. I won't be here when he learns how demoralizing it can be to argue with a stubborn, obstinate child, how it undermines your confidence as a parent.

Dennis will be a mess and he knows it. I am afraid of that. Regretful to leave him to fend for himself: eat alone, stay up all night alone, wander around the house that we so love and revel in together.

I don't want to die and disappear. I want to live, and live each day grateful that I am alive. But knowing that I don't have much time left means every single second is precious and meaningful, and must not be wasted.

One Last Thing: Night Terrors

I had a terrifying childhood, yet no one in my family knew. I was especially terrified at night. I secretly was afraid of the bomb at the top of the steps. Every night, when my sister accompanied me up to my room at bedtime, I was petrified by the reflections on doorknobs, and so my mother would cover all of the knobs with rags or towels. I had an ungodly fear of the lights from cars that would flash through my bedroom through the Venetian blinds. Surely, I thought, those light strips will decapitate me.

My nightmares were so frightening that I often woke up screaming. No one ever reassured me. No one ever said: "It's alright, the lights from the cars are just the headlights reflecting on walls." Or, "There are no bombs in the house." No one informed me that doorknobs could not hurt me.

I spent my Saturday afternoons at the movies watching scary double feature films, and I remember them all: *The Blob* (at age five), *The Incredible Shrinking Man* (age six), *The Fly* (also age 6), *The She-Devils* (age seven). Even *Pinocchio* was terrifying. These upsetting thoughts were all in my own private small-child brain. Raw fear, with never an explanation or a reassurance.

I was always expected to smile at all relatives, friends, teachers, strangers, and cashiers—anyone whose path I crossed. No grumpy faces allowed. No being disgruntled in any situation. Accommodation, acceptance, and enthusiasm were the expectation. I felt I had no choice. The mandate was to "be cheerful."

The fears and the expectation of constant cheerfulness culminated in a dramatic event: my grandmother's murder and her funeral when I was ten. It was too horrific a death for anyone in my family to address directly, even though it was on the front page of the city newspaper. I had to accompany my mother to the morgue.

Now, with a terminal cancer diagnosis, I am brought full circle. I have new fears, and I still feel the expectation to be positive. And my fears? Surprisingly, it's not death. It's pain. And procedures like the coffinlike MRI. I still feel the mandate to be positive, *and I know how to do that*. But here's what's different. I'm not alone with my fears. I have Dennis.

Dear Mila

I always wanted a girl. Everyone who knows me knows this. I never had a daughter, but now I have a granddaughter. I love buying dresses for little girls! I especially love buying dresses for you, Mila. I have explained this fixation to your parents: it's not that I have this idea of girls as frilly Disney princesses. It's that, when I was a little girl, I got *one new dress a year*. I got it in September, for my birthday, and it was to be worn on the first day of school. It was purchased at the famous and historic Wanamaker's department store. My one dress a year.

When you read this, I will be gone. Maybe, though, you will read about my resistance to being categorized, tamped down, demoralized, undone, or diminished. I don't necessarily advocate lying or forging signatures unless it is the *only means necessary*. Which it was for me. I do advocate you continue to do the things you love to do. Right now it's reading, building, drawing. Do all the things you love to do, Mila—with gusto, with heart, with joy.

You were born into a family with much creativity and an abundance of mechanical ability as well. My dad was an excellent cartoonist and writer. Your grandfather Dennis's dad built his house from the ground up while raising four children. He also was a calligrapher. His wife, your great-grandmother, Theresa, loved to arrange flowers. Maggie's dad is famous for his humorous writing and wit. Your Nana Jeanne has a passion for animals and liberal causes. Grandpa Dennis, Uncle Sam, and your dad, Jesse, can draw anything and build anything. They are logical and focused thinkers. I have already seen this trait in you when you play. You seem to be on a mission. I was always on a mission, too! My mission was to get educated and have only sweet, pure love in my life, which I did. I hope you will always have loving experiences as well. Of course, I think that Jesse and Maggie are the perfect parents. I know your parents love you very much.

You like to bounce, jump, run around with a fantasy cape, shouting, "Make way for ducklings." Remember, my sweet Mila, you are a San Francisco native and that has meaning, even though you live in Boston now. Grandpa and I loved the six months we had "Mila Mondays," walking around Golden Gate Park with you in the stroller. It was our favorite day of the week.

I love that you are getting to know some of your cousins. I loved most of my cousins and am still close to a few of them. You have Genevieve and Graham, Jill and Jason's children, who live nearby. And you have Henry and Eliza, Julia and Dave's kids; and Laura's new baby, born in August 2018. So you are in good shape in the cousins department. Family is important.

I was a "silly girl" and for a long time I thought that was a stupid trait to have. Your dad Jesse is "silly" too! It is **not** a stupid trait. Silly is good! If you feel silly, go big! Same with love, work, travel, ideas, making things, thinking up things, drawing things, planting things, confiding in friends in an intimate way. Do it up! This is your life, my darling Mila. When you meet your sister (I say this as a "little sister" myself), take care to bring her along—but also see who she is too.

I love you more than you can ever know. Love, Nana Jan.

Jani's Scrapbook

Top: Jan, age 9, with her mother and sister Faye at Spring Lake, New Jersey, a beach near Philadelphia. Bottom: Jan, age 6, with her father and sister Faye on the Atlantic City boardwalk.

Mae (top row second from left) and Jan (top row, fourth from left), age 8, at their neighborhood day camp.

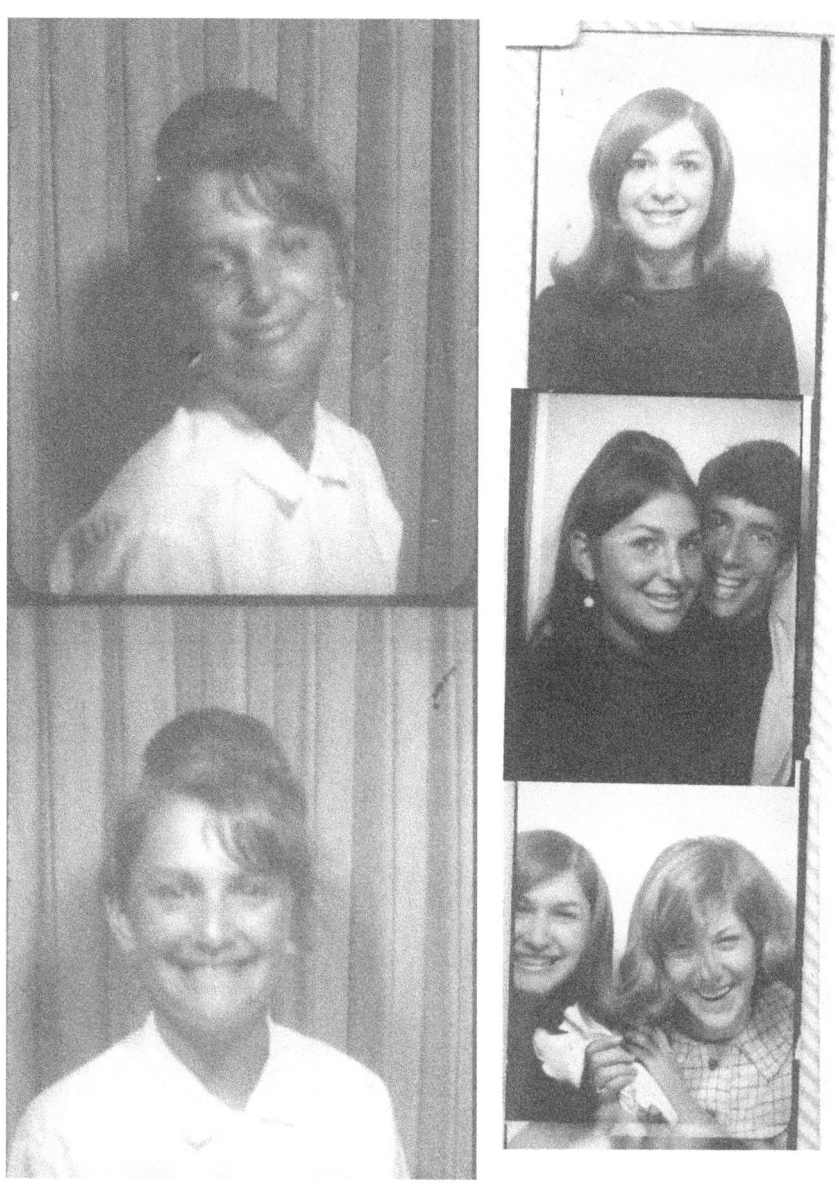

Teenage Jan liked to vamp and act silly in photo booths.

Jan's athleticism, outgoing personality and beautiful smile won her a coveted spot on the cheerleading team at Northeast High School in Philadelphia. The photo was taken from the front of Jan's childhood home, a typical Philadelphia row house.

Jan dressed up for a costume party with her prom date and longtime friend Bobby Caplan.

Jan, 1968, dressed for her prom. She loved the styling of this made-in-Paris dress.

Jan, 2017, at a Halloween party, beaming, delighted to wear her prom dress again.

Top: Jan receiving her MA in Psychology at San Francisco State University in 1982. Bottom: Jan receiving her PhD from Northern California Graduate University in 1995.

Jan in her Psychotherapy office in Noe Valley 2015. Becoming a psychotherapist had been a dream of Jan's since she saw an adaptation of psychologist Dr. Robert Linder's book "The 50-Minute Hour" on the television series "Playhouse 90" when she was seven years old.

Dennis and Janice were married in their back yard in Noe Valley, San Francisco on June 6, 1982. Jan interrupts her wedding ceremony for an aside to the audience.

Jan, Dennis, Jesse, and Sam at the beach along the California coast.

Top: Jan and Jesse at the mother and son dance in high school. Bottom: Jan and Jesse after Jesse grew 8 inches in his sophomore year in high school.

Top: Jan visiting Sam at the University of Bologna, Italy where he spent his junior year of college. Bottom: A joyful Jan embracing Sam.

Jan and Dennis, 1996, camping with the children when they were young. Bottom (L): Jan and Dennis, 1985, shortly after they were married. (R): Jan bicycling with Dennis (2014) in Santiago, Chile where Dennis often worked.

Top Left to right: Jesse and his wife Maggie, Sam with fiancée Gina, Jan and Dennis. Bottom: Jan with her granddaughter Mila.

Jan, effervescent and elegant.